'NI

~~~~~~ waterways
regulations

(the CEVNI Rules explained)

**Written by Tam Murrell**

*Edited by Jon Mendez*
*Proof Reading: Alan Thatcher*
*Illustrations by Pete Galvin*
*Photos: Tam Murrell*
*Layout: Creativebyte*
*Printed through: World Print*

We recommend that you
carry the relevant navigation
handbook on board for the
areas you intend to cruise.

Published by
**The Royal Yachting Association**
RYA House, Ensign Way
Hamble, Southampton SO31 4YA
Tel: 0845 345 0400  Fax: 0845 345 0329
Email: info@rya.org.uk  Web: www.rya.org.uk

The RYA is committed to encouraging both women and men
to participate in boating.
For clarity only, the text in this handbook is written using the
masculine gender eg. Man Overboard.

A cruise through the Inland waterways of Europe can be a most delightful experience, made much more pleasant by having the additional confidence of knowing the rules.

The CEVNI code provides a set of signs, rules and procedures for navigating the Inland Waterways of Europe which are heavily utilised by commercial traffic whose operators are well aware of the CEVNI requirements. They also have an expectation that all other boat operators will know the score and understand what is going on. Knowing the CEVNI regulations is the best way of protecting yourselves and your boat.

Whilst a CEVNI qualification and carrying the CEVNI rule book onboard happens to be a legal requirement, there is no reason why learning shouldn't be easy. This new RYA CEVNI book provides all the information you need in a clear and concise way.

The CEVNI code is used as the basis for a number of country specific regulations such as: for navigation on the Rhine, navigation in France and Holland. Visitors to these countries and their waterways will need to make themselves aware of any local requirements and there are a number of books and cruising guides available which cover these.

Some of the CEVNI rules have caused great confusion in the past; such as the meaning of a 'normal vessel' and does that mean a pleasure craft? Another is Left bank and Right bank and their relationship to buoyage. The RYA CEVNI book will make these things crystal clear, enabling a successful CEVNI examination and is an extremely useful reference book to have onboard.

Enjoy the book, enjoy the learning and enjoy the cruising on the Inland Waterways of Europe

S Carr

Stuart Carruthers RYA Cruising Manager

CEVNI (Code Européen des Voies de Navigation Intérieure) is the Code governing navigation on all the interconnected European inland waterways. These rules apply inland of the line defining the seaward limit of each country's waterways. They were originally devised by the United Nations in 1985 so that boatmen of all nationalities can communicate with each other and understand what is going on without necessarily speaking each other's language.

CEVNI is the basis for the various countries' own regulations such as the Règlement Général de Police in France and Belgium, the Binnenvaartpolitiereglement in Holland, and the Règlement de Police pour la Navigation du Rhin for Rhine areas.

Local regulations may differ in some respects from the basic CEVNI regulations to deal with more specific situations. However, knowledge and understanding of CEVNI is an essential pre-requisite for anyone cruising on the continental mainland.

Many local variations are included in this book, but the most notable exceptions at present are Belarus, Kazakhstan, the Republic of Moldova, the Russian Federation, and Ukraine. If you are planning to visit these countries you should familiarise yourself with the many specific requirements in force there. As CEVNI becomes progressively more integrated with national regulations it is likely that many local variants will disappear.

Over the past few years there has been a big increase in the number of pleasure craft using European inland waters for their own sake, rather than as a short cut to the Mediterranean. These are often vessels such as narrowboats, wide-beam cruisers, and new-build or converted Dutch barges, many of which fall outside the definition of Small Craft and are expected to comply fully with the requirements. If they remain in European waters longer than as a visitor they will also generally be expected to comply with equipment requirements (such as having a blue board and an all-round yellow horn light) which may not have been necessary in the vessel's home country.

**Boatmaster**
The person who has all the necessary qualifications and is in charge of the vessel.

**Vessel**
Any craft on inland waterways including Small Craft, ferries, floating equipment and sea-going vessels.

**Normal vessel**
The Code refers to Normal Rules, and Small Craft are generally exempt from these. Normal Vessel means any vessel other than Small Craft.

**Small Craft**
Vessels under 20m long, other than tugs, ferries, and boats licensed to carry more than 12 passengers. (Some authorities use 15m as the cut-off, and France uses 20 displacement tonnes).

**Motorised Vessel**
Any vessel proceeding with its own mechanical means of propulsion.

**Sailing Vessel**
Any vessel proceeding under sail only. If using auxiliary engine it is considered to be a Motorised Vessel.

**Floating Equipment**
Floating machinery, such as dredgers, elevators, cranes, etc.

**Floating Installation**
A fixed floating structure, e.g. floating dock, landing stage, etc.

**Floating Material**
Any raft or object capable of navigation, other than a vessel or floating installation.

**Ferry**
Vessel providing transport across a waterway.

**Convoy**
Tug and barges under tow or being pushed, or vessels coupled side by side.

**Berthing**
To make fast directly or indirectly to the bank or bed of the navigation.

**Left Bank** (also Left-Hand Side)
The bank on the left-hand side as you look downstream (downhill on a canal).

**Right Bank** (also Right-Hand Side)
The bank on the right-hand side as you look downstream (downhill on a canal).

On summit levels of canals, and on broad waterways and lakes, the terms left and right are defined by the relevant authorities.

For the purposes of CEVNI, waterways are divided into two classes:
**Class 1**   Normally rivers
**Class 2**   Canals, lakes, and broad waterways

*The CEVNI Rules are normally laid out so a boatmaster has to search through to find out how to make a particular manoeuvre before he makes it. This book does not follow the original sequence of the CEVNI rules and is designed to be a quick, user friendly and straightforward reference. Whilst all reasonable care has been taken, neither the RYA nor the author can be held liable for any misinterpretations that might occur.*

## Boatmaster

The Boatmaster is responsible for the vessel. He must hold all the necessary qualifications and ensure the regulations are complied with at all times.

Even in the absence of specific rules, the boatmaster must exercise vigilance and good practice to avoid damage to vessels, banks, works, etc., of any kind.

He must take every step to avoid imminent danger, even if this entails departure from the regulations.

If a nearby vessel needs assistance, the boatmaster must give immediate aid commensurate with the safety of his own vessel.

Boatmaster and crew must not navigate if their abilities are impaired by tiredness or intoxication.

## Crew

Crew members must carry out the boatmaster's orders and assist in compliance of the regulations.

There must be sufficient skilled crew to ensure the safety of the vessel and everyone on board.

The helmsman must be suitably qualified and over 16 years old.

## Vessels

A vessel's dimensions and speed must be suitable for the waterway it is on. It should not be overloaded in any way.

The helmsman must have a clear view in all directions and be able to hear sound signals. If necessary, fit mirrors or other aids for clear, all round visibility. If circumstances require it, a look-out must be posted. The helmsman must be able to communicate with crew positions at all times.

The ship's registration documents and a current copy of the regulations for the relevant waterways must be kept on board.

Some countries require Normal Vessels to keep a log.

The vessel's name and registry details should be marked indelibly fore and aft on the outside of the hull in letters at least 20cm high; on Small Craft 10cm, with no requirement for marking on the stern. The owner's name and address should also be displayed conspicuously. Tenders must be identified. On Normal Vessels, anchors must be indelibly marked with the name or number of the vessel.

Every vessel with a draught of 1m or more must have draught marks permanently inscribed on the hull at maximum 5cm intervals.

If your vessel goes aground or sinks, inform the authorities immediately. Someone must stay on board, or nearby, until authorised to leave. If the vessel is a hazard to navigation, warn other vessels in time for them to take avoiding action. Endeavour to clear the channel as quickly as possible.

## Protection of the waterway

It is prohibited to allow any object which could cause damage to project beyond the sides of the vessel.

Anchors when stowed must not project below the bottom of the vessel.

If a potentially hazardous object falls from the vessel, inform the authorities at once and, if possible, mark the spot.

If an unknown obstacle is encountered, inform the authorities at once, detailing its position as accurately as possible.

It is prohibited to tie up to waterway signs or marker buoys, or to damage them in any way. Should damage occur, or be noticed, inform the authorities immediately. The same applies to damage to permanent structures such as locks and bridges, etc.

It is prohibited to throw, or allow to fall, into the water any hazardous substances, particularly petroleum products. In the event of accidental spillage, inform the authorities immediately, specifying the type of spillage and exact location.

Vessels must not be washed, or painted, with prohibited substances.

Household refuse, sewage residues, contaminated bilge water or other special wastes, may only be disposed of at appropriate reception facilities. Domestic waste water may only be discharged in accordance with national regulations.

## PROHIBITIONS

**General no entry/no passage**
*can be indicated by a sign, red lights, boards or flags*

**Short-term stoppage**

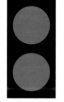

**Prolonged stoppage**
*(e.g. a lock which is out of action)*

**Short-term stoppage**

**Prolonged stoppage**
*(e.g a lock is out of action)*

**No entry except for non-motorised small craft**

**No overtaking**

**No overtaking for convoys over 110m x 12m**

**No passing or overtaking**
*(effectively one-way traffic here)*

**No berthing**

**No berthing within a lateral distance of (e.g. 40) metres out from sign**

**No anchoring**

**No mooring**

**No turning**

**Do not make wash**

 or   or

**No passage outside the marked area**

**No passage, but prepare to get underway-**
*(one of two red lights goes out)*

**No entry to a port or sidearm**

**Signs mounted on certain craft**

**Boarding prohibited**

**No smoking**

25

**Lateral berthing prohibited within (e.g. 25) metres**

## OTHER TRAFFIC LIGHTS

or (isophase flashing)

Two flashing yellow lights signal that a craft is coming out of a port or sidearm. Traffic on the main waterway must alter course or speed accordingly. In France, one flashing yellow is also used. One flashing yellow means entry into that same port or sidearm is forbidden. Two yellows signify entry is permitted, but with great caution.

**Recommendation to steer from the fixed white light towards the isophase flashing one**

White lights also give advance warning of difficulty ahead

 or  or

**Stop as required by the regulations**

**You may proceed**

## Movable bridges

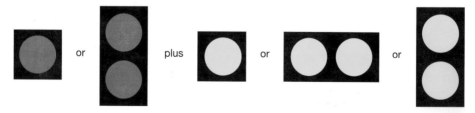

Passage at movable bridges is controlled by red and green lights. If yellow lights show at the same time as one or two reds, passage is permitted for vessels of reduced height. One yellow signifies two-way traffic. Two yellows signify one-way traffic.

## MANDATORY

**Go in direction indicated by the arrow**

**Channel moves to port**

**Channel moves to starboard**

**Keep to port side of channel**

**Keep to starboard side of channel**

**Cross channel to port**
*(this shows you will be meeting other vessels starboard to starboard and should display a blue board - see Rules of the Road)*

**Cross channel to starboard**
*(upstream traffic gives priority to downstream traffic during these two crossing manoeuvres)*

**Stop as necessary**

**Do not exceed (e.g.12) km/h**

**Sound your horn**

**Keep a sharp lookout**

**Do not enter, or cross, the main waterway if this obliges other vessels to alter course or speed**

**Make VHF contact on ship-to-ship channel**
*(normally 10)*

**Make VHF contact on channel indicated**

*Normal Vessels are required to have two VHF radios; one is ordinarily kept on the ship-to-ship Channel (10) and the other on the local nautical information channel. Vessels should announce their presence on the ship-to-ship channel when entering blind sections, narrow channels or bridge openings.*

## RESTRICTIONS

**Depth of water limited**

**Headroom limited**

**Width of passage or channel limited**

**There are restrictions on navigation - make enquiries**

**Channel is (e.g. 40) metres from the bank**

**Transverse current** *(to be introduced)*

## RECOMMENDATIONS

**Recommended passage**

**Two way traffic**

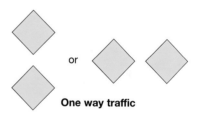

or

**One way traffic**

The recommended arch or span through a fixed bridge may be marked by yellow diamonds (or occasionally by yellow lights). If there is a recommended passage, craft use unmarked spans at their own risk.

*If you see two yellow diamonds, traffic is one-way, in your favour. There will be a 'no entry' sign on the other side. If you see only one yellow diamond, there will also be one on the other side, permitting two-way traffic.*

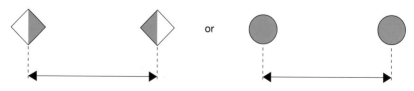

or

**Recommendation to keep within the space indicated**

**Recommendation to follow direction of the arrow**

## GENERAL AUTHORISATION TO PASS

can be indicated by sign, flags, green lights or boards

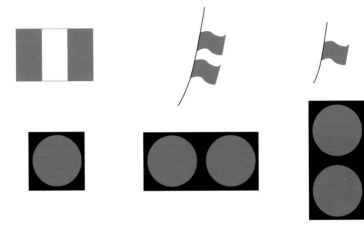

## INDICATIONS

**Entry permitted to a port or sidearm**

**Overhead cable**

**Weir**

**Ferry not operating independently**

**Self propelled ferry**

**Berthing permitted**

**Anchoring permitted**

**Mooring permitted**

**Mooring only for putting vehicles on or off**

**Berthing permitted within a lateral distance of (e.g. 60) metres out from the sign**

**Berthing permitted within a lateral distance of between (e.g. 30 - 60) metres out from the sign**

**Maximum number of vessels permitted to berth abreast**

**Berthing reserved for various categories of commercial craft** (may have additional marking on the white shape)

**Turning area**

**You are on the major route**

**Major route ahead**

**End of prohibition or obligation**

**Drinking water**

**Telephone**

**VHF channel in local use**

## MANY SIGNS MAY HAVE EXPLANATORY OR SUPPLEMENTARY PANELS ATTACHED FOR EXAMPLE

**Speed limit 10kph in 1000m**

**Stop if necessary - ferry ahead**

**No berthing for 1000m in direction of the arrow**

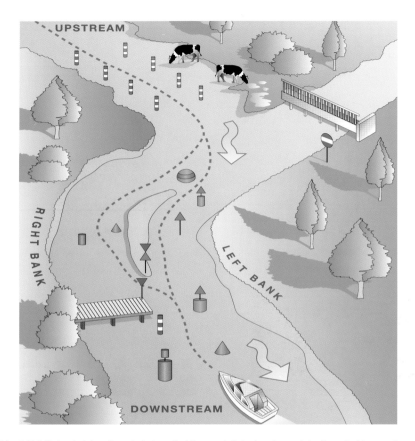

Within CEVNI the left bank or left-hand side, and right bank or right-hand side are from the perspective of a person looking downstream, or looking downhill on a canal.

IALA European buoyage uses red buoys to mark the port side of the channel when coming from the sea, and green buoys to mark the starboard side. As you cross the seaward limit or pass through a lock the buoyage continues using red and green in the same manner as you travel upstream or uphill, i.e. red to port and green to starboard.

When these two differing frames of reference coincide it means that the red/port buoys are on the 'right hand side' of the waterway - they become the right bank of the channel.

Green and red buoys are often found inland used in isolation to steer craft away from a particular obstruction.

On channel markers, old buoyage may still be encountered which uses black instead of green.

## CHANNEL MARKS

**Left-hand side of the channel**
Green conical buoys, or buoys/spars with a conical topmark. May have rhythmic green light and radar reflector.

**Right-hand side of the channel**
Red cylindrical buoys, or buoys/spars with a cylindrical topmark. May have rhythmic red light and radar reflector.

A white letter P on a green or red buoy means that the channel is next to a berthing area. If it has a light it will flash at a different rhythm to other buoys marking the channel.

**Bifurcation of the channel**
Red and green horizontal striped spherical buoys, or buoys/spars with a spherical topmark. May have continuous quick, isophase or group flashing white light and radar reflector.

**Main channel**
The main channel may be indicated by the addition of a green cone or red cylinder with appropriate rhythmic green or red light.

### Land marks
These are marks on top of posts. May have rhythmic green or red lights fitted.

 or        or

**Channel is close to left bank**              **Channel is close to right bank**

## Cross-overs

Where the channel crosses from one bank to the other, you will see a post with one of these topmarks:

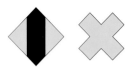

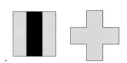

**Left bank marks**
May have a yellow flashing or occulting lights with an odd number characteristic (other than 3).

**Right bank marks**
May have a yellow flashing or occulting lights with an even number characteristic (other than 2).

*simple cross-over*

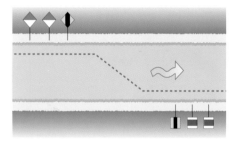

*long cross-overs*

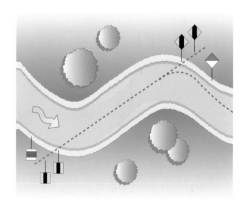

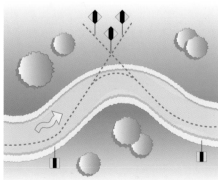

## OBSTACLE MARKS

### Fixed marks

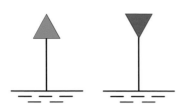

Fixed marks are cones or triangular boards on a post. Left-hand marks are green and point up. Right-hand ones are red and point down. They may have rhythmic green or red lights.

Bifurcations are red over green cones/triangles. May have a continuous, quick isophase, or group flashing (3) white lights.

Bank walls on the approaches to secondary arms, waterways, or harbour entrances may be marked as far as the dividing mole by these marks. Vessels entering harbour are regarded as upstream traffic.

### Buoyage

**Left-hand**
Green/white horizontal striped spars or spar buoys with a green cone topmark. They may have rhythmic green lights and generally have a radar reflector.

**Right-hand**
Red/white horizontal striped spars or spar buoys with a red cylinder topmark. They may have rhythmic red lights and generally have a radar reflector.

## ADDITIONAL MARKS FOR NAVIGATION BY RADAR

### Bridge piers

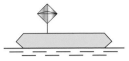

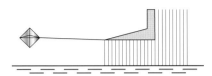

May be marked by yellow floats carrying a radar reflector

or by a radar reflector on a pole, upstream and downstream of the piers.

### Overhead cables

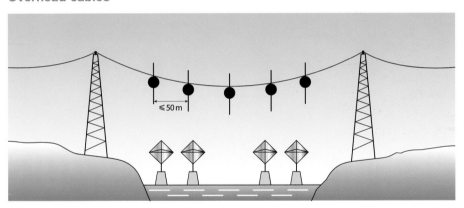

≤ 50 m

Overhead cables may be marked by radar reflectors attached to the cable at max. 50m apart. The radar image will be seen as a series of points to identify the cable.

They may also be marked by radar reflectors on yellow floats, arranged in pairs, near each bank, each giving a radar image of two points side-by-side to identify the cable.

### FLOOD MARKS

Certain rivers use flood marks bearing a reference level and a Roman numeral. Some rivers are closed to navigation when Level II is reached. On others, such as the Moselle for instance, it is Level III.

## ADDITIONAL BUOYAGE & MARKS ON LAKES AND BROAD WATERS

### Cardinal marks

The four quadrants North, East, South, and West are bounded by the true bearings NW-NE, NE-SE, SE-SW, SW-NW, taken from the point of interest.

The cardinal mark is named after the quadrant in which it is placed, and indicates that the mark should be passed on the side of the quadrant named.

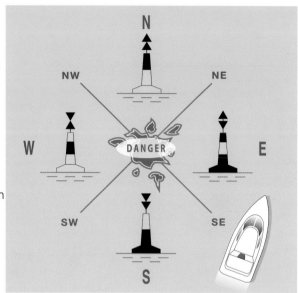

### *Lights*

Lights, if fitted, are white

**North Cardinal**  Continuous quick or very quick light.
**East Cardinal**  Group flashing (3) quick or very quick lights.
**South Cardinal**  Group flashing (6) quick or very quick followed by one long light.
**West Cardinal**  Group flashing (9) quick or very quick light.

### Isolated danger marks

Erected on, or moored above, an isolated danger which has safe water all around it.

May have white group flashing (2) lights.

### Safe water marks

Mark the axis or middle of a channel, or a landfall.

Lights, if fitted, are white isophase, single-occulting, one long flash/10secs, or Morse Code A (one short one long).

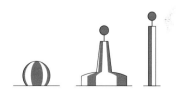

## Weather warnings on lakes

**Caution warning:** A yellow light with about 40 flashes/minute indicates the probable onset of a dangerous phenomenon at an unspecified time.

**Danger warning**: A yellow light with about 90 flashes/minute indicates the imminent arrival of a dangerous phenomenon.

### Restricted areas

Marked by yellow buoys, possibly with a yellow X topmark.  Lights, if fitted, are yellow.  Rhythm will be different from that on other foregoing buoyage for lakes.  As far as possible, the nature of the restriction or prohibition will be made clear on charts,

by markings on the buoy, or by signage on the bank.

A zone where navigation is totally prohibited may be marked by a rigid red pennant on the buoys.

If a prohibited or restricted area is crossed by a channel permitting vessels to pass, the upper half of the two buoys at the entrance may be coloured red on the right-hand side of the entrance and green on the left-hand side, as seen by the boatmaster leaving the channel.

In France, spherical yellow buoys are generally used to mark an area reserved for bathing.  Conical buoys delineate one form of activity from another.

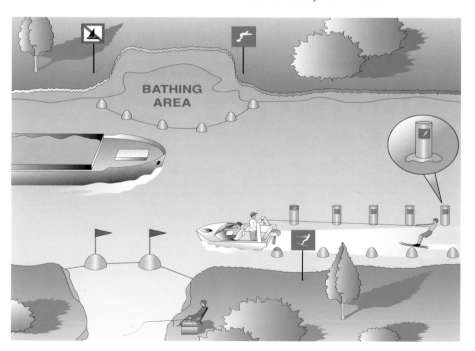

## Authorised

**Motorised craft**

**Pleasure craft**

**Waterskiing**

**Sailing**

**Rowing boats and canoes**

**Windsurfing**

**High speed boats**

**Launching**

**Personal watercraft**

## Forbidden

**Motorised craft**

**Pleasure craft**

**Waterskiing**

**Sailing**

**Rowing boats and canoes**

**Windsurfing**

**High speed boats**

**Launching**

**Personal watercraft**

# SOUND SIGNALS

Most sound signals are different from those used at sea or on the UK inland waterways.

A short blast is about one second, and a long blast four seconds, with about one second between each blast.

A 'series of very short blasts' is six or more $1/4$ second blasts with about $1/4$ second between each blast.

A bell peal is about four seconds, and can also be made by banging two pieces of metal together.

It is prohibited to use signals other than those laid down, and these may only be used as defined.

Sound signals by convoys will be given by the vessel carrying the boatmaster.

Normal Vessels have an all-round yellow light synchronised with the horn.

Small Craft are exempt from many of the rules, and give way to Normal Vessels. It follows therefore that they may sound only a limited number of general signals, detailed below:

Signals which are authorised for use by Small Craft are shown coloured blue in this table and black elsewhere in the book.

I am steering to (or holding to) starboard
I am steering to (or holding to) port
I am going astern
I am unable to manoeuvre
Do not overtake me
Imminent danger of collision (six or more very short blasts)

Caution
I am turning (or turning about) to starboard
I am turning (or turning about) to port
I wish to overtake on your starboard side
I wish to overtake on your port side
I am exiting from a port or side arm and crossing the waterway
I am exiting/entering a port or side arm and turning to starboard
I am exiting/entering a port or side arm and turning to port

DISTRESS SIGNALS
........ repeated long blasts on the horn or
........ by ringing of a bell = distress signal

*In Holland four short blasts followed by one long signifies* "I am in need of medical assistance" *and the morse signal K [ ■■ ■■ ■■ ] is traditionally used for* "Please open the bridge".

Vessels underway in reduced visibility should adjust speed to suit the conditions and circumstances. Unless waived by the authorities, you should have a radio capable of communications with other craft, and with shore based stations. Post a look-out on the bow who can communicate with the helmsman. The vessel must make the prescribed sound signals, and carry the relevant lights.

If you can no longer proceed in safety, stop.

Vessels proceeding using radar should take account of the reduced visibility of other vessels.

When stopping, vessels must keep as clear of the channel as possible.

When meeting another vessel keep as far to starboard as necessary and passport to port.

Stationary vessels, (including vessels aground), in or near the channel, outside a harbour or designated berthing area, must make a sound signal when they hear an approaching vessel.

**On Class 1 waterways** (rivers), this will be one bell peal each minute for a vessel on the right-hand side of the channel, and two bell peals for a vessel on the left-hand side. A vessel uncertain of its position will sound three bell peals.

**If stationary on Class 2 waterways** (canals, lakes and broad waterways), all vessels will sound one bell each minute. Some authorities permit the horn signal ■ ■ ■ instead. A vessel not lying parallel to the channel or otherwise is a potential danger and shall give this signal even when it cannot hear any approaching vessel's signal.

## SOUND SIGNALS

■ A single vessel (other than a downstream vessel navigating by radar) sounds one long blast once every minute. So too do all vessels underway using radar on Class 2 waterways.

■ ■ A towed convoy or boats abreast under way (other than downstream vessels navigating by radar) sound two long blasts once every minute (or one blast if using radar on Class 2 waterways).

Vessels (other than Small Craft) travelling downstream and navigating under radar sound a series of three ascending tones (e.g. doh-re-mi) three times in succession, with a total length of two seconds. This is repeated as often as necessary.

## NAVIGATING BY RADAR

In circumstances where navigation would be impossible without radar there must be two persons conversant with radar navigation on board.

A vessel is exempt from having a look-out posted if the helmsman is able to hear sound signals from other craft.

If a vessel, which is seen as a potential danger, does not respond to radio calls, the boatmaster should take steps in good time to avoid collision.

In all situations, when approaching another vessel, slow down and, if necessary, stop.

Under radar, only overtake another vessel if you have agreed the overtaking side by radio and the channel is sufficiently wide.

If you see on your radar screen a vessel whose movements or position might lead to danger, or if you approach a section where there may be vessels, not yet visible on your screen, the following actions must be taken:

**On Class 1 waterways,** if travelling downstream, a Normal Vessel will sound its tri-tone signal as often as necessary. It must reduce speed, and stop if necessary.

If travelling upstream, vessels sound one long blast (two long blasts if they are a towed convoy or boats abreast). They must call the other vessel by radio and announce their name, what type of vessel they are, their position, direction, and side they propose to pass. They must reduce speed, and, if necessary, stop.

The downstream vessel will then reply giving the same information, and confirm the side for passing or indicate the other. A Small Craft will give the same information but simply announce the side on which it is giving way.

**On Class 2 waterways**, in either direction, sound one long blast, and repeat as often as necessary. Communicate by radio with the oncoming vessel giving all information for safe navigation. Reduce speed and, if necessary, stop. (Note: In France, vessels use one or two long blasts according to whether they are a single vessel or a convoy/travelling abreast, and regardless of their use of radar).

Small Craft should state they are Small Craft and the side on which they are giving way.

Ferries should sound one long blast followed by four short, and state they are a ferry and the course they are taking for their crossing.

## NAVIGATING WITHOUT RADAR

Vessels should sound one or two long blasts every minute as required for their category of vessel. If on a Class 1 waterway you hear the tri-tone signal, clear the channel as fully and quickly as possible, and if necessary, stop until the other vessel has passed.

Ferries should sound one long blast followed by four short.

If you hear a fog signal ahead of the beam, slow down to the minimum required for safe steerage and, if necessary, stop or turn.

## RADIO

Radio telephone equipment must be of an approved type and used in accordance with the relevant regulations.

Motor Vessels, other than Small Craft, ferries and floating equipment, should have two radios, one tuned to the navigation information channel and the other to the ship-to-ship channel (CH10).

Vessels should announce their presence before entering blind sections, narrow channels, or bridge openings. Vessels should state the type of vessel they are, their direction of travel and their position.

## DEFINITIONS

For the purpose of CEVNI, waterways are divided into two classes:

| | |
|---|---|
| CLASS 1 waterways | Normally rivers |
| CLASS 2 waterways | Canals, lakes and broad waterways |
| UPSTREAM | Towards the source of the river, or, on a canal, uphill through the locks. On the summit level of a canal, 'upstream' is determined by the canal authorities. |
| MEETING | Two vessels travelling on courses directly opposed to each other. |
| OVERTAKING | A vessel comes from behind another vessel and overtakes it. |
| CROSSING | Two vessels are approaching each other in any other manner other than meeting or overtaking. |
| GIVE-WAY VESSEL | The vessel which, when two vessels are meeting or crossing, must give way to the other. |
| STAND-ON VESSEL | The vessel which, when two vessels are meeting or crossing, maintains its course and speed. |

## GENERAL PRINCIPLES

Meeting or overtaking is permitted only when the channel is unquestionably wide enough for safe, simultaneous passage.

Vessels should not change their course or speed in a manner which might lead to danger of collision.

If collision cannot be avoided solely by the action of the give-way vessel, the stand-on vessel must manoeuvre to avoid collision.

## LAKES

On lakes, the steerage rules are the same as those for the prevention of collisions at sea. Apart from certain passenger vessels, Normal Vessels or commercial vessels DO NOT have the absolute priority they enjoy on rivers and canals but must give way to sail and unpowered craft.

## SMALL CRAFT

The term 'Small Craft' in this section includes towed convoys and vessels abreast if comprised wholly of Small Craft.

Small Craft give absolute priority to all other craft, with the exception of hydrofoils and hovercraft.

Unless any specific rule states otherwise, Small Craft must give all other craft (except hydrofoils and hovercraft) enough room to hold their course or to manoeuvre.

It follows, therefore, that many of the rules applicable to Normal Vessels do not apply to Small Craft. It is however essential that the helmsman of a Small Craft understands what a Normal Vessel is doing.

### Small Craft between themselves

#### *Crossing and meeting*

A motorised Small Craft gives way to all other Small Craft, and a Small Craft without an engine gives way to a Small Craft under sail.

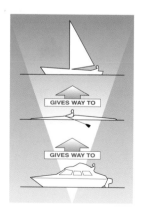

When two small motorised craft are crossing; the vessel which has the other on its starboard side gives way. However, a Small Craft on the starboard side of a marked channel should maintain its course.

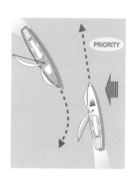

When two small sailing craft are crossing or meeting they follow the rules set out for normal sailing craft.

When two small motorised craft meet and there may be a danger of collision, each steers starboard to pass to port.

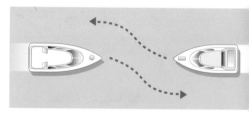

#### *Meeting in narrow channels*

A Small Craft travelling upstream gives way to one travelling downstream.

When upstream is not defined, the stand-on vessel is the Small Craft with no obstacle to starboard or with the outside of a bend to starboard.

However, a motorised Small Craft normally gives way to a Small Craft under sail.

*Overtaking*

Generally, the Small Craft which is overtaking passes to port of the vessel being overtaken.

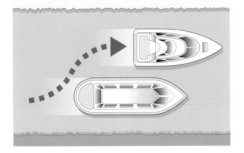

If the channel is unquestionably wide enough the vessel may overtake on the starboard side. It shall not oblige the overtaken craft to change its course or speed.

A Small Craft under sail and overtaking another generally passes on the side to which the overtaken vessel has the wind.

A Small Craft being overtaken by a Small Craft under sail should allow it to overtake on the side on which the wind is coming from (the windward side).

*Entering and exiting ports and side-arms*

Small Craft shall not turn about or exit/enter any port or side-arm if such manoeuvre is likely to oblige other vessels, including other Small Craft, to change their course or speed.

## GENERAL RULES

### Normal crossing rules

When two Normal Vessels are crossing and there is danger of collision, the vessel which has the other to starboard shall give way.

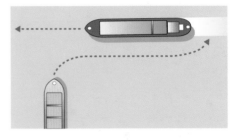

However, a vessel on the starboard side of a marked channel should maintain its course.

The foregoing rule shall not apply if one of the vessels is turning, leaving a berth, or entering/exiting a port or side-arm.

It should perhaps be reiterated that all Small Craft, including those under sail, give way to Normal Vessels. Small Craft are defined by size, not by function. A pleasure craft over 20m will therefore be classed as a Normal Vessel along with cargo carriers, passenger boats and other working craft.

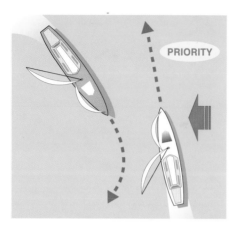

PRIORITY

When two vessels under sail are crossing, the vessel with the wind on its starboard side has priority.

If they both have the wind on the same side, the give-way vessel is the one to windward.

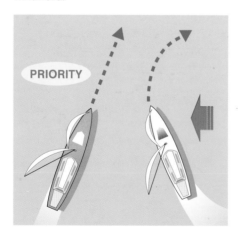

PRIORITY

If a vessel with the wind to port cannot determine whether the crossing vessel has the wind to port or starboard, it shall give way.

## Normal meeting rules

### Class 1 waterways

Normal Vessels travelling upstream give way to those travelling downstream.

If the upstream vessel wishes to leave the downstream vessel a course to pass to port, he gives no signal.

If he wishes to leave the downstream vessel a course to pass starboard to starboard he displays on his starboard side, by day, a bright scintillating white light, and/or a blue board, or a blue flag. By night, he displays a scintillating white light, and possibly also a blue board.

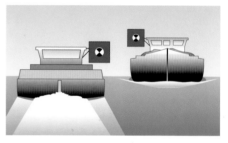

For simplicity the term 'blue board' will now be used to include the various visual signals.

If the upstream vessel thinks that the downstream vessel has not understood his intentions, he will give one short blast if he is leaving a passage to port, and two short blasts if he is leaving a passage to starboard.

Downhill vessels shall take the course indicated by the upstream vessel, and repeat the visual or sound signals made by the upstream vessel.

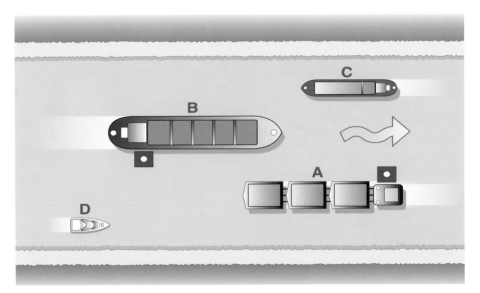

*The Pusher (A) travelling upstream is 'blue-boarding' the Barge (B) travelling downstream in the middle. The Barge acknowledges this and they pass starboard-to-starboard. The Barge (C) shows no signal as he is passing in the normal way, port-to-port. The Small Craft (D) simply keeps out of the way.*

However, if a passenger vessel travelling downstream wants to call at a landing stage on the side used by the upstream vessel, or a towed convoy moving downstream wants to keep close to a particular bank, it has the right to ask the upstream vessel to change course using the signals as described above.

If the upstream vessel sees that the course requested by the downstream one will cause danger of collision it will sound a series of very short blasts. The helmsman will then take all necessary steps to avoid the danger.

### Class 2 waterways

When two vessels meet and there is any risk of collision each shall veer to starboard, thus passing port-to-port. However, if both vessels are under sail the rules regarding sailing vessels apply.

In exceptional cases, vessels may ask to pass starboard to starboard. They will sound two short blasts and display their 'blue board'. The other vessel will respond with the same signal and leave necessary space to starboard.

These signals will be retracted after the meeting unless it is necessary to continue passing vessels to starboard.

If a vessel sees that the course requested will cause danger of collision it will sound a series of very short blasts. The helmsman will then take all necessary steps to obviate the danger.

## Meeting vessels towed from the bank

If a vessel meets another being towed from the bank, it passes on the side away from the towline.

## Meeting in narrow channels

On waterways where 'upstream' and 'downstream' are defined, if an upstream vessel sees a downstream vessel approaching a narrow channel, it shall stop and wait until the downstream vessel has passed.

A downstream vessel which can see that an upstream vessel has already entered the narrow channel shall stop above the channel until the vessel has passed.

When 'upstream' and 'downstream' are not defined, the Normal Vessel with no obstacle to starboard, or with the outside of a bend to starboard, shall hold its course and other vessels should wait until it has passed. If two Normal sailing vessels or two Small Craft under sail meet, the vessel to windward, or if both are navigating with the wind, the vessel with the wind on its starboard side maintains its course, and the other vessel waits until it has cleared the narrow channel.

If there is restricted view of the channel, a vessel shall sound one long blast before entering, and as often as necessary while proceeding.

When meeting in a narrow channel is inevitable, vessels shall ensure they pass at a point, and in a manner, to minimise

danger. If there is danger of collision a series of very short blasts should be sounded

## Meeting prohibited by signs

**A4**

Where meeting is prohibited by sign A4 the rules for meeting in narrow channels apply.

Where a one-way traffic system is in force, prohibition of passage is indicated by signs A1, and authorisation by signs E1.

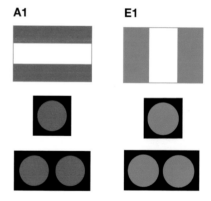

## Overtaking

Overtaking is permitted only if it can be carried out without danger. The overtaken vessel shall slow down if necessary to make the procedure quick and safe.

Vessels will generally overtake on the port side of the overtaken vessel, but can do so to starboard if the channel is sufficiently wide.

If the overtaken vessel is required to alter course, or it appears not to have noticed the overtaking vessel, the overtaking vessel sounds two long blasts followed by two short blasts to pass to port, and two long blasts followed by one short blast to pass to starboard.

If the overtaken vessel agrees to this, it sounds one short blast to be overtaken to port, and two short blasts to be overtaken to starboard.

If overtaking is not possible on the side requested, the overtaken vessel sounds one short blast if it is possible to overtake to port, and two short blasts if it is possible to overtake to starboard. The overtaking vessel then sounds one or two short blasts as appropriate to signal its change of direction.

When overtaking cannot be carried out without danger the vessel to be overtaken sounds five short blasts.

An overtaking vessel under sail shall generally pass on the side on which the overtaken vessel has the wind. The overtaken vessel should facilitate this.

Small Craft cannot ask Normal Vessels to change course to permit overtaking.

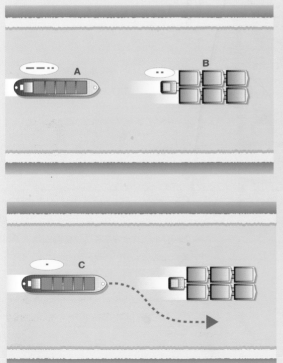

(A) The motor barge sounds two long and two short blasts to signal he wishes to overtake to port of the pusher. (Two long mean "I wish to overtake", and two short mean "I am steering to port").

(B) The pusher replies with two short blasts, saying this is not possible, (effectively saying "I am steering to port") with the consequence that the give-way vessel behind him cannot then come through on that side.

(C) The motor barge then sounds one short blast to signal he wishes to overtake to starboard instead. The pusher will not now give any further signal unless there is any doubt about what is happening.

Overtaking is prohibited generally on sections marked by the sign A2 or A4. Overtaking between convoys (where at least one is pushed and >110m x 12m) is prohibited on sections marked by A3.

**A2**          **A3**          **A4**

*On the Rhône, a vessel displays a blue flag at the bow (or all-round white light at night) when overtaking.*

## Sections with a prescribed course

These are marked by signs B1, B2, B3 or B4. **B1**

**B2**          **B3**          **B4**

**B3a**          **B3b**          **B4b**

Vessels travelling upstream shall not impede the progress of downstream vessels whilst manoeuvring in accordance with these signs.

## Turning and leaving or joining a waterway

Turning, leaving berths or anchorages, or entering/exiting harbours and side-arms can only be carried out without obliging other vessels to change course or speed abruptly.

### Turning

A vessel which requires other vessels to alter course or speed so it can turn, sounds one long blast, followed by one short, to signal turning to starboard, or two short to signal turning to port. Other vessels shall then facilitate the turn, particularly when the turning vessel needs to turn up into the current.

Turning at approved turning places is bound by these same rules.

### Vessels leaving a berth or anchorage

A vessel which requires other vessels to alter course or speed so it can leave a berth or anchorage, sounds one short blast when vessels are approaching on its starboard side, and two short blasts when vessels are approaching on its port side.

Approaching vessels shall then facilitate

## Entering and exiting harbours and side arms

A downstream vessel wanting to turn upstream to enter a harbour or side-arm must give priority to an upstream vessel which also wishes to enter the same harbour or side-arm.

If it requires other vessels to alter course or speed, the manoeuvring vessel, when entering or leaving, shall sound three long blasts, followed by one short if turning to starboard, or by two short if turning to port.

If after leaving it wishes to cross the waterway it sounds three long blasts. Before completing the crossing, it then sounds one long followed by one short to turn to starboard, or one long followed by two short to turn to port.

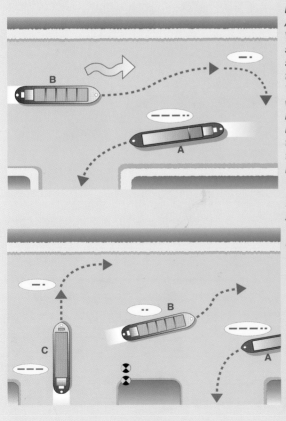

*ENTERING AND EXITING PORTS AND SIDE ARMS*
*Vessel (A) travelling upstream signals three long blasts and two short to indicate he is turning into the side-arm.*
*Vessel (B) coming downstream also wishes to enter this arm. Vessel (B) must give priority to Vessel (A) before he signals to say he is turning about. He too will then give the three long/two short signal as he is about to enter the arm.*

*ENTERING AND EXITING PORTS AND SIDE ARMS*
*Vessel (A) signals three long blasts and two short to indicate he is turning into the side-arm.*
*Vessel (B) sounds two short blasts to say he is moving to port, out of the way.*
*Vessel (C) sounds three long blasts to say he is entering the main waterway and crossing it. He then sounds one long blast and one short to indicate he is turning to starboard. Two flashing yellow lights at the entrance also warn craft of his entry into the main waterway.*

Other vessels modify their course and speed as necessary, whether or not the harbour/side-arm is controlled by yellow flashing lights.

If the signs below are used, vessels may not leave the harbour/side-arm if Normal Vessels on the main waterway would need to modify their course or speed.

Exit from a harbour/side-arm may be controlled by red and green traffic lights. If passage is permitted by the appropriate green signal, other vessels modify their course or speed to facilitate this.

### Other steerage rules

Vessels may travel abreast only if there is sufficient room to do so in safety.

Except when overtaking or meeting, it is prohibited to navigate within 50m of vessels displaying two or three blue cones by day, (or two or three all-round blue lights at night).

*In France, this is one or two red cones by day, one all-round red or two alternating flashing red lights at night.*

It is prohibited to go alongside a vessel under way without permission of its boatmaster.

Trailing anchors, cables or chains is prohibited.

Drifting is prohibited.

Vessels must regulate their speed and not create excessive wash likely to cause damage to other vessels or structures.

When encountering any of the general 'no passage' signs (see p.8) vessels must stop short of the sign.

## PASSAGE THROUGH BRIDGES

Unless there is sufficient width for simultaneous passage of two or more vessels, the rules for passage of narrow channels apply (see p.28).

Passage may be marked by signs A10 prohibiting navigation outside of the area between the two signs, or D2 recommending that vessels remain within the area between the two signs.

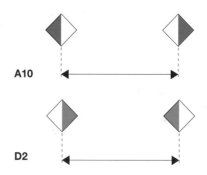

### Fixed bridges

Prohibited spans of fixed bridges may be marked by no entry signs or lights A1.

Other spans may be marked by yellow diamonds to signify they are the preferred openings. One yellow diamond signifies it is open to traffic in each direction. Two yellow diamonds indicate that it is closed to traffic from the other direction.

Unmarked openings may be used at the boatmaster's own risk.

### Movable bridges

Obey any instructions given by bridge staff.

Slow down on approach

If you cannot or do not wish to proceed stop short of any 'stop' sign.

Overtaking on the approach is prohibited.

Passage may be regulated by traffic lights:

- one or more reds signify passage prohibited

- red and green in conjunction alert vessels to be prepared to pass.

- one or more green signal that passage is permitted.

Two red lights, one over the other, signify

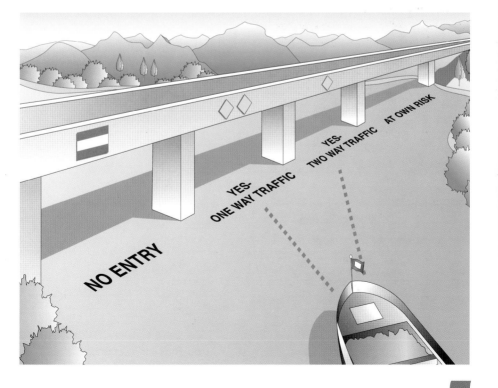

that navigation is suspended. However, a yellow light in conjunction with one or two reds allows passage by vessels of restricted airdraught (one yellow signifies passage in each direction, and two signifies passage prohibited in the other direction).

Red, green, or yellow boards may be used instead of lights.

## WEIRS

Trailing of anchors, cables or chains near a weir is prohibited.

Passage through an opening in a weir is permitted where you see green signs E1, (or yellow D1 if there is an overhead bridge).

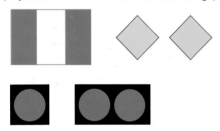

Passage is prohibited if any general red signs A1 are displayed.

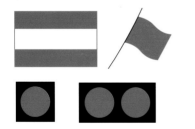

## PASSAGE THROUGH LOCKS

A vessel must slow down when arriving at a lock. If it cannot, or does not wish to proceed, it must stop short of any 'stop' sign. Overtaking in lock approaches is prohibited.

Boatmasters must communicate by VHF on the channel assigned to the lock.

Passage through a lock is in order of arrival. However, Small Craft are not entitled to a separate locking. They must wait until they are asked to enter by the lock staff. If locking through with Normal Vessels, Small Craft must enter the lock last, and keep clear of the Normal Vessels.

However, certain vessels have priority of passage, and fly a long red pennant at the bow to signify this. They will generally be vessels of the navigation authority, fire, police, customs etc, or passenger boats on a public service. France also allows priority to tugs without a convoy, and sea-going ships.

### In a lock

- Anchors must be fully raised.
- Vessels must avoid knocking against any part of the lock or other vessels.
- Vessels must keep within any limits marked on the lock walls.
- Vessels shall be made fast until allowed to leave.
- Fenders are mandatory, and must be floating ones if movable.

- Vessels must not discharge water onto the copings or other vessels.

- Unless otherwise permitted, use of the engine is prohibited from the time the vessel is made fast until it leaves the lock.

It is obligatory to keep at least 10m from a vessel carrying inflammable materials (displaying a blue cone or light). These vessels will not be locked through at the same time as a passenger vessel.

Vessels carrying two or three blue cones/lights (one or two reds in France) are locked separately.

To ensure safe and orderly navigation, lock staff may give instructions which vary from these provisions. All vessels must comply with such instruction.

## Visual Signals

Entering and leaving locks is regulated by visual signals:

- Red and white boards A1 or red lights signify entry/exit prohibited.

- Two red lights one above the other signify 'lock out of service'.

- Green in conjunction with red, or one of a pair of reds becoming extinguished signify 'prepare to enter'.

- Green and white boards E1 or green lights signify 'entry/exit permitted'.

- In the absence of lights/boards, entry/exit is prohibited unless permitted by lock staff.

*In France, where the smaller Freycinet locks are often automatic and boater-operated, lock failure can be caused by two or more Small Craft working through together.*

*As the first boat enters the chamber, the control light goes to red. Any subsequent craft is then entering against a red light, leading to complications of the operating electronics. To compound the problem, Small Craft frequently enter the lock with a gap between each craft, but leave bunched up together. This means the electronics register a lesser number of craft leaving. No other craft can then use the lock until maintenance staff sort out the problem!*

A vessel is berthed when it is directly or indirectly moored to the bank, or at anchor.

A vessel should berth as close to the bank as possible and not obstruct navigation in any way.

Vessels should be berthed to allow for changes in water level and wind, and the suction and wash of passing vessels.

Vessels must not use trees, railings, posts, metal steps and handrails, etc. for making fast or warping.

Berthing is prohibited within:

- 10m of a vessel carrying one blue cone/light.

- 50m of a vessel carrying two blue cones/lights (two red cones, two alternating flashing all-round red lights in France).

- 100m of a vessel carrying three blue cones/lights (one red cone/all-round red light in France).

A vessel berthed in the channel (or a vessel carrying dangerous substances berthed at any place) must maintain a permanent watch on board.

SUR 50 METRES

PROMENEURS, PECHEURS,
A PARTIR DE CE POINT ET SUR UNE DISTANCE DE 50 M.
IL EST INTERDIT DE S'ARRETER

## AREAS WHERE BERTHING IS PROHIBITED

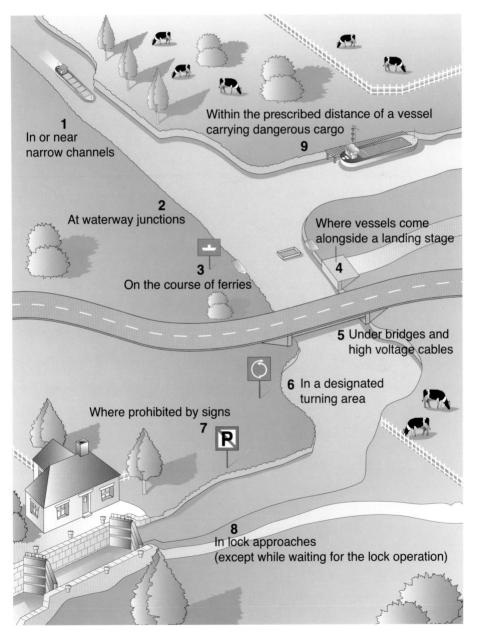

**1** In or near narrow channels

Within the prescribed distance of a vessel carrying dangerous cargo **9**

**2** At waterway junctions

**3** On the course of ferries

Where vessels come alongside a landing stage **4**

**5** Under bridges and high voltage cables

**6** In a designated turning area

Where prohibited by signs **7**

**8** In lock approaches (except while waiting for the lock operation)

41

## Masthead light

Strong white light projecting an uninterrupted beam forward through 225° to 22° 30' abaft the beam.

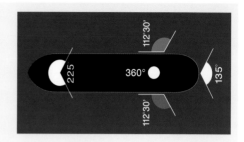

## Side lights

Bright green to starboard and bright red to port projecting an uninterrupted beam through 112° 30' to 22° 30' abaft the beam

## Stern light

Ordinary or bright white light projecting an uninterrupted beam aft through 135° to 22° 30' abaft the beam on both sides.

## All round light

Light projecting an uninterrupted beam through 360°.

Lights prescribed for use at night are to be used in all conditions of poor visibility.

## VESSELS UNDER WAY

(except when carrying dangerous cargo)

### A single motorised Normal Vessel

Shows no day marks*. At night it carries a white masthead light, side lights which are below and behind the masthead, and a stern light.

It may carry a second masthead light, higher than and aft of the first. This is mandatory on vessels over 110m.

*In Belgium, all vessels under way must fly a red flag with a white square in the centre on a mast.*

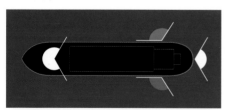

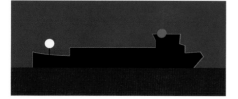

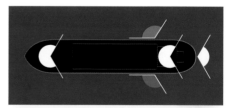

## Motorised Small Craft

At night, a motorised Small Craft shows the same lights as a single Normal Vessel.

The side lights may be together in one lamp. The masthead and stern lights may similarly be together in one lamp, at the mast – effectively an all-round white.

The above applies also to Small Craft towing or abreast of other Small Craft. When in tow, or abreast of a Normal Vessel (other than as a tender) a Small Craft carries an all-round white light.

Motorised Small Craft under 7m require only an all-round white light.

## Sailing Vessel

At night, a sailing vessel shows side lights and stern light only. It may in addition carry at its mast an all-round red over an all-round green.

If motor-sailing by day it shows, as high as possible, a black cone pointing down, and by night the same lights as an isolated motor vessel of the same size.

## Small Craft neither Motorised nor Under Sail

A sailing craft under 7m only needs an all-round white light, but should display a second white light upon the approach of another vessel.

Proceeding alone, this Small Craft should display an all-round white light. A ship's tender only displays this light upon the approach of another vessel.

## A Motorised Vessel leading a towed convoy

By day, a Motorised Vessel leading a towed convoy, or acting as an auxiliary for another Motorised Vessel, displays a yellow cylinder with black and white stripes at each end. If more than one vessel leads the convoy, each vessel carries the cylinder.

By night, such vessels show two masthead lights, one above the other, and side lights. Its stern light is yellow. If more than one vessel leads the convoy, each carries three masthead lights.

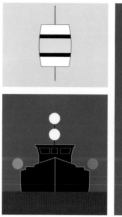

## Vessels under tow

By day, vessels under tow display a yellow ball, and by night an all-round white light. The last vessel in the convoy also shows a white stern light.

If any section of the convoy is over 110m long, it carries two yellow balls or all-round white lights, one at each end.

If the rearmnost section comprises two or more craft abreast, only the two outside vessels carry white stern lights. (If the rearmost craft are Small Craft they are discounted in this context).

A Motorised Vessel under way, and temporarily preceded by an auxilliary motor vessel, displays a yellow ball by day. At night, it shows the lights of a single motor vessel under way.

Ships under tow display a yellow ball by day, but may show their side lights instead of an all-round white at night.

## Pushed convoys

A pushed convoy carries three masthead lights on the bow of the leading vessel (on pushed vessels abreast, the vessel on the port side carries three masthead lights), arranged in a triangle with the point uppermost.

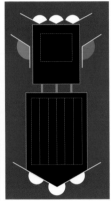

Any other vessel whose full width is visible from ahead carries a white masthead light, lower than the triangle of lights.

Side lights are shown at the widest part of the convoy, as near to the pusher as possible.

The pusher itself displays three white stern lights in a horizontal line, and every vessel whose full width is visible from the stern shows a white stern light.

If more than two pushed vessels are so visible, only the two outside ones show the stern light.

If the convoy is preceded at night by one or more auxiliary vessels, the stern lights of the pusher will be yellow. By day, the pusher carries a yellow ball.

If a convoy is pushed by two pushers abreast, the one on the starboard side carries the three stern lights, while the one to port carries only a single stern light.

Pushers up to 110m x 12m are considered to be a single motor vessel (92m x 9.5m in France).

## Side-by-side formations

Vessels travelling abreast each show the usual navigation lights, except that the side lights will only be shown at the outside of the formation.

If one of the vessels is unpowered, it shows an all-round light at the mast instead of a sectored one. If preceded by an auxiliary Motorised Vessel they show the same lights, but by day, show a yellow ball.

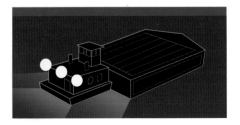
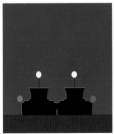
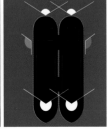

## Passenger vessels

By day, passenger vessels under 20m licensed to carry more than 12 passengers display a yellow bicone visible from all directions.

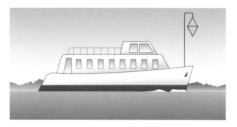

## Ferries

***Ferries not moving independently*** show a green ball visible from all directions by day and an all-round green light over an all-round white at night.

***The lead boat of a longitudinal-cable ferry*** displays at night an all-round white light visible from all directions.

***Ferries moving independently*** show a green ball by day. By night they show an all-round green light over an all-round white, plus the side and stern lights of a Normal Vessel.

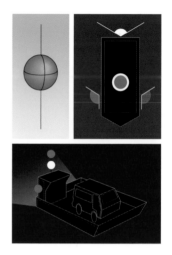

***Ferries moving independently and enjoying priority*** show additionally by day a white cylinder below the green ball. Additionally, at night, they show a second all-round green light above the first.

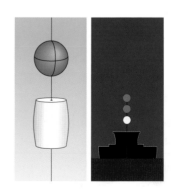

**Vessels enjoying priority of passage** at specified places show a red pennant at the bow in addition to any other prescribed marks.

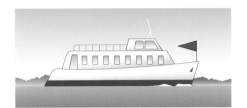

### Floating installations and assemblies of floating materials

under way at night show sufficient all-round white lights to define their shape and size.

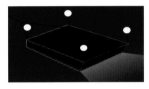

### Vessels unable to manoeuvre

By day, a red flag may be swung from side to side, or two black balls are shown, visible all round, one above the other. By night, it shows two all-round red lights one above the other, or a red light swung from side to side.

A Small Craft may use a swung white light instead.

Craft will also give the sound signal four short blasts as required.

**Vessels with limited ability to manoeuvre** when carrying out works such as cable laying, etc, will show in addition to other prescribed markings:

- By night, three all-round lights, i.e. an all-round red over an all-round white over an all-round red.
- By day, a black ball over a black bicone over a black ball.

If their operations cause obstruction they shall additionally show:

- By night, two all-round red lights, one above the other on the side(s) where the obstruction occurs, and two all-round green lights, one above the other, on the side(s) where the channel is clear.
- By day, two black balls one above the other on the side(s) where the obstruction occurs, and two black bicones one above the other on the side(s) where the channel is clear.

These provisions do not apply to floating equipment at work when stationary.

## Vessels carrying dangerous cargo

By day, vessels carrying dangerous cargo show one, two or three blue cones, point downwards and high enough to be visible.

By night, they show one, two or three all-round blue lights. These cones and lights are additional to any other marks or lights prescribed for the category of craft, e.g. the masthead light, side lights and stern light of a Normal Vessel.

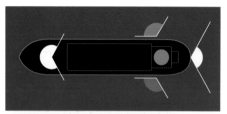

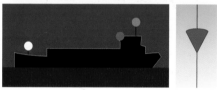

- Vessels carrying inflammable materials are defined by one blue cone/light.
- Vessels carrying materials constituting a health hazard are defined by two blue cones/lights.
- Vessels carrying explosives are defined by three blue cones/lights.

If dangerous cargo is carried by a pusher unit it is the pusher that displays the cones/lights, or the motorised vessel of a side-by-side formation. If there are two pushers the shapes/lights are shown by the starboard pusher.

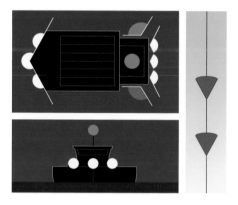

These cones and lights continue to be shown when a craft carrying dangerous cargo is moored or at anchor. They are then in addition to the various lights and shapes for each particular type of stationary vessel.

Sea-going ships operating temporarily on inland waters may instead display an all-round red light by night and a red swallowtail pennant (code flag B) by day.

*In France, the two blue cones/lights are replaced in the day by two red cones and at night by two alternating flashing all-round red lights. The three blue cones/lights are replaced by one red cone/light. In the case of pushed or towed convoys each vessel shows the appropriate lights/cones.*

## STATIONARY VESSELS

(except when carrying dangerous cargo)

### Vessel moored to the bank

At night, vessels moored directly or indirectly to the bank show an all-round white light on the side nearest to the channel. Some vessels, Small Craft in particular, may be exempt from this requirement if it is obviously not necessary.

Craft may show two all-round whites, one at the bow and one at the stern, on the side nearest to the channel.

### A vessel stationary offshore

A vessel stationary offshore (including those at anchor) without direct or indirect access to the bank shows a black ball, visible all-round by day. At night it shows two all-round whites, one at the bow and a lower one at the stern.

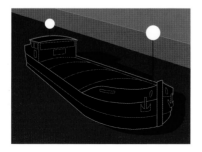

### A pushed convoy stationary offshore

By day, a pushed convoy stationary offshore shows a black ball, visible all-round on the pusher and on the leading vessel or outermost leading vessels of the convoy. By night, it shows an all-round white on each vessel of the convoy, with a maximum requirement of four such lights, providing the outline of the convoy is clearly defined.

### Small craft

Small Craft show an all-round white light in any suitable position.

### Ferries not moving independently

when moored at their landing stage by night show an all-round green light over an all-round white. The lead boat of a longitudinal-cable ferry carries an all-round white light visible from all directions.

### Ferries moving independently

When moored at their landing stage by night they show an all-round green light over an all-round white. When they cease operation they extinguish the green all-round light.

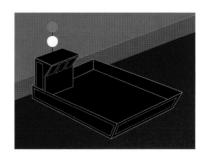

## Floating installations and assemblies of floating material

Stationary at night show sufficient all-round white lights to define their shape and size.

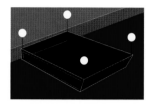

## Floating equipment at work, and grounded or sunken vessels

- On the side(s) on which the channel is clear, by day, two green bicones are shown one above the other, visible all-round, replaced at night by two all-round green lights.
- On the side on which the channel is not clear by day, a red ball visible all-round, replaced at night by an all-round red light.

- The day symbols may be replaced by the general green/white 'passage permitted' and red/white 'no passage' boards.

### Vessels protected against wash

- On the side(s) on which the channel is clear, by day a red flag over a white one, or one flag with a red upper half and white lower is shown. These are replaced at night by one all-round red light over one all-round white.
- On the side on which the channel is not clear, by day a red ball visible all round is shown, replaced at night by an all-round red light.

- The day symbols may be replaced by boards with the same colour characteristics.

---

Seriously damaged vessels, those engaged in rescue work, unable to manoeuvre, or specifically authorised, are the only craft which may be so protected. It is important not to confuse the red over white board/flags signifying that passage is permitted without making a wash with the red/white/red horizontal striped 'no entry' signal!

## Anchoring

A vessel at anchor shall exhibit where it can best be seen, in the fore part an all round white light or one black ball. Vessels over 50m shall exhibit a second white light at a lower level near the stern.

### Anchors presenting a danger to navigation

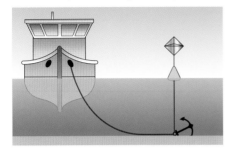 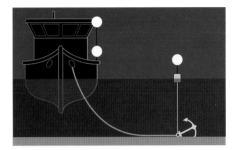

Vessels and assemblies of floating material or floating installations whose anchors may cause danger to navigation, at night replace the all-round white light nearest to the anchor with two all-round white lights, one above the other. The anchor itself is marked by an all-round white light.

By day, the anchor is marked by a yellow float with a radar reflector.

## VESSELS ON SPECIAL ACTIVITY
### Fishing Vessels

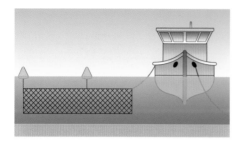 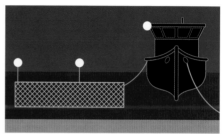

When stationary, with nets or poles extending into or near the channel, the nets/poles are marked by day with yellow floats sufficient to show their position. By night, the yellow floats are replaced by all-round white lights.

- In addition to other relevant marks, a trawler when working displays, by night, two all-round lights, green over white. The green light is lower than the masthead light and the white light higher than the side lights. A trawler under 50m does not require a masthead light. By day, a trawler displays two black cones one above the other, point to point.

- Other fishing boats show these same lights and shapes except that the all-round green is replaced by all-round red, and any masthead light is extinguished.

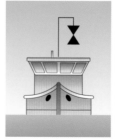 

If fishing boats have tackle extending more than 150m horizontally from the side of the vessel, they additionally display on the tackle side, by day, a black cone pointed upwards and, by night, an all round white light lower than the other all round white light but higher than the side lights.

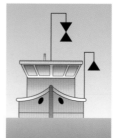 

## Vessels engaged in minesweeping

In addition to other relevant marks, a vessel engaged in minesweeping shows by night three all-round green lights in a triangle, point upwards on the topmast. By day, these are replaced by three black balls in a similar pattern.

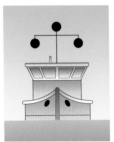 

## Fire fighting and other official vessels

May show, in addition to other relevant symbols, an all-round scintillating blue light by night and by day.

## Vessels carrying out work and under way

Show in addition to other relevant symbols an all-round scintillating yellow light, by night and day.

## Vessels used for diving

 Show a rigid reproduction of Code flag A. They may show the various signals for a vessel unable to manoeuvre.

Other vessels shall keep at least 50m (or such other distance as determined) from vessels engaged in diving. Sports diving shall not be practised on the route of a ferry, at harbour entrances or areas reserved for water skiing.

*In France a red flag with a white diagonal line or white diagonal cross may sometimes be used.*

## Pilot Vessels

At night instead of an ordinary masthead light shall show two all-round lights one above the other, white over red.

## DISTRESS SIGNALS

In addition to, or instead of, the various relevant sound signals the following visual distress signals may be used:

- a flag or other suitable object waved in a circle
- a light waved in a circle
- a flag having above it or below it a ball or similar shape
- rockets or shells throwing red stars fired into the air
- red flare
- flames from burning tar, oil etc
- a flashed light signal SOS in Morse Code  ■■■ ▬ ▬ ▬ ■■■
- slow repeated up-and-down movements of the arms to each side.

### ABOUT THE AUTHOR
Tam Murrell has been boating for business and pleasure since the late 50's. As owner and operator of commercial vessels ranging from working narrowboats and barges on UK inland waters to small coasters trading in and around the Thames estuary and into northern Europe he has a wide experience of handling craft in a variety of contexts. Since 1995 he and Di, his wife, have spent much of their time on continental waterways on their 24m Dutch barge, and run a barge-handling school in France for RYA and French qualifications.

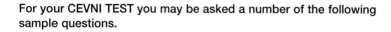

**For your CEVNI TEST you may be asked a number of the following sample questions.**

---

One of these need not be carried on board

   a.  Boat Certificate of Registry
   b.  Navigation Regulations
   c.  Credit cards
   d.  VHF Licence

---

On a vessel this means:

   a.  I have a diver down
   b.  Under 20m carrying more than 12 passengers
   c.  Restricted in ability to manoeuvre
   d.  Constrained by draught

---

On a vessel pushing this means:

   a.  Fishing
   b.  Pilot on board
   c.  Not under command
   d.  Carrying inflammable materials

---

A vessel showing this means:

   a.  I wish to communicate with you
   b.  Vessel enjoying priority of passage
   c.  I require medical assistance
   d.  I have a diver down

---

An upstream vessel showing this means:

   a.  I am stopping
   b.  I am going astern
   c.  I am leaving a course for downstream
      vessels to starboard
   d.  Stop

---

What are the meanings of these signs:

   a.  No entry
   b.  Barge ahead
   c.  Keep a sharp lookout
   d.  Sound your horn

---

a. Sign on left hand bank - cross over to right
b. Sign on right hand bank - cross over to left
c. Keep in centre of channel
d. No mooring

a. Enter
b. Do not enter
c. Enter with caution
d. Keep a sharp lookout

a. Sign on right hand bank - cross over to left
b. Sign on left hand bank - cross over to right
c. Keep in centre of channel
d. No mooring

a. Customs
b. Harbour Office
c. No anchoring
d. Lock

a. You must berth within 500m of the sign
b. No berthing in direction of arrow for 500m
c. Berths for 500 vessels
d. Width of channel 500cm

a. No entry
b. Channel close to left bank
c. Channel close to right bank
d. Channel in centre

a. No entry
b. Channel close to left bank
c. Channel close to right bank
d. Channel in centre

This sound signals means:

a. Turning to starboard
b. Turning to port
c. Imminent danger of collision
d. Astern propulsion

This vessel is

a. Not under command
b. Restricted in ability to manoeuvre
c. A motorised vessel leading a towed convoy
d. Constrained by draught

This vessel is:

a. Motor sailing
b. Carrying materials constituting a health hazard
c. Fishing
d. Turning to the south

This shape means:

a. A pilot vessel
b. Towing
c. Fishing
d. A ferry

a. Windsurfing permitted
b. Windsurfing forbidden
c. Recreation area
d. Permission required to windsurf

a. Keep to port
b. Keep to starboard
c. No entry except for non-motorised small craft
d. Moorings ahead

a. No power vessels
b. Disengage propeller
c. Authorised passage for motorised craft this channel
d. Keep a lookout for power vessels

a. Stop as necessary
b. Keep a sharp lookout
c. Low bridge
d. Go astern

a. Overtake here
b. No overtaking
c. Use both sides of channel
d. No entry

a. Enter
b. Authorised passage, one-way traffic
c. Stop
d. Keep a sharp lookout

a. Strong current
b. Bends in river
c. Do not create wash which could damage banks and structures
d. No mooring

a. Do not enter
b. Recommended passage, one-way traffic in this direction
c. No mooring
d. Request permission before entering this area

a. No entry
b. Channel close to left bank
c. Channel close to right bank
d. Channel in centre

a. No entry
b. Channel close to left bank
c. Channel close to right bank
d. Channel in centre

# THE CEVNI TEST

A Normal Vessel as opposed to a small vessel is:

    a. Over 10m in length
    b. Over 13.7m in length
    c. Over 20m in length
    d. Over 80 tonnes

The meaning of this signal is:

    a. A vessel under sail
    b. A fishing vessel
    c. A vessel towing
    d. A vessel motor-sailing

A vessel showing this signal is:

    a. Fishing
    b. Being towed
    c. Carrying materials constituting a health hazard
    d. Sailing

What does the signal on this vessel mean:

    a. Vessel protected against wash, clear channel is shown by a red flag over a white flag
    b. Do not pass on either side
    c. Pass either side
    d. Pilot on board

A vessel showing this signal is:

    a. Aground
    b. At anchor
    c. Carrying dangerous cargo
    d. Not under command

Which of the following statements are true:

    a. Small craft are not permitted on Class 1 waterways
    b. Small craft are not permitted on Class 2 waterways
    c. Small craft must always give way to Normal Vessels
    d. Small craft must always carry a pilot

What does this sign mean:

    a. No passing or overtaking
    b. Two way traffic
    c. Pass port-to-port in this section
    d. Do not pass port-to-port in this section

What does this sign mean:

a. No entry
b. No speed limit
c. Sound horn
d. Keep a sharp lookout

Does this sign on a bridge span mean:

a. Recommended passage two-way traffic
b. Recommended route for normal vessels only
c. Recommended route for small vessels only
d. Do not pass under this span

What does this sign mean:

a. Environmentally sensitive area
b. Keep to starboard
c. Authorised passage, one-way traffic
d. Keep to mid channel

On which side should this buoy be kept when going downstream:

a. To the North
b. To the east
c. To port
d. To starboard

In this situation, involving two small craft, which of them should keep clear:

When overtaking in a river, would you pass:

a. On the starboard side of the other vessel
b. On either side of the vessel
c. On the side on which the other vessel is displaying a blue board
d. On the side on which you are displaying a blue board

A sound signal of three short bursts means:

a. I am turning to starboard
b. I am going astern
c. I am the third vessel in a tow
d. I am unable to manoeuvre

In October 1998, the UN Economic Commission for Europe Resolution number 40, 'International Certificate for Operators of Pleasure Craft', was adopted. The RYA introduced this on behalf of the European Boating Association and it took five years of negotiation before the resolution was passed. The end result is the 'new' International Certificate of Competence (ICC), which has been issued since April 1999.

Prior to this, the RYA issued the Helmsman's Overseas Certificate (HOC) and latterly the 'old' International Certificate of Competence. The main difference with the new ICC, is that competence in boat handling, navigation and knowledge of the collision regulations (Rules of the Road), must be proven by test or a previous qualification. Also the CEVNI test must be taken if the inland waters endorsement is required. CEVNI is the acronym for Code Européen des Voies de Navigation Intérieure. The lack of a test on the CEVNI regulations was the major sticking point for acceptance by other European countries, who were simply not happy with such a system.

Generally, an ICC is required when navigating the inland waterways of Europe, the main notable exception is The Netherlands. In The Netherlands an ICC is only required by vessels that are either longer than 15 metres and/or capable of more than 20kph (11 knots). If cruising to Europe to explore the canals and rivers, both categories 'coastal' and 'inland' will be required and so the CEVNI test, as well as proof of general boat handling competence, is needed.

For coastal areas in Northern Europe and Scandinavia, the ICC is generally not required. Again, there are exceptions and these include Poland and the Baltic States of Lithuania, Estonia and Latvia. It is also useful to have one in Germany. Conversely, in the Mediterranean an ICC is usually required, particularly in Italy, Greece, Croatia and Turkey. ICCs are not required in Spain on British flagged yachts. However, Spanish harbour masters and other officials are used to their own nationals having to be licensed so it can be difficult to persuade them British flagged vessels do not require them. You either have to be prepared to stand your ground and argue the case or you may decide that it is easier to actually have an ICC. Portugal does require skippers to hold the ICC.

When applying for an ICC there are a number of choices to be made. Firstly, the waters on which the boat is to be used must be specified. The choice is 'inland' and 'coastal' and both or either can be chosen.

If 'inland' is chosen, either alone or together with 'coastal', the CEVNI test must be taken and signed off on the application form. This also applies to those who are renewing existing ICCs or Helmsman's Overseas Certificates. It is important to note that no other RYA or UK professional maritime qualification test CEVNI and so even holders of those tickets must take the test to obtain the 'inland' endorsement.

The second choice is the type of craft for which the ICC will be used. The choice is 'power' and 'sail'. It is important to note that a sailing vessel with an auxiliary engine requires both categories.

When the ICC application form is submitted, either a practical test must be signed off by an RYA Teaching Centre, or evidence of competence enclosed. The accepted evidences of competence are listed in full on the last page of the ICC application form, but basically a course completion certificate for Day Skipper practical or above is sufficient evidence for operating a sailing vessel with an auxiliary

engine. For motor cruisers Day Skipper (Power) is acceptable and for small motor boats, Ribs etc Power Boat Level 2 or above is required. A photocopy of the course completion certificate or certificate of competence should be included with the application form.

The RYA is the UK issuing authority for the ICC. You can obtain an ICC form by visiting the RYA website: www.RYA.org.uk or telephone 0845 345 0370. You can also find details of RYA Teaching Centres on our website.

Complete the application form and send it to RYA House together with a passport sized photograph and photocopies of practical course completion certificates, if applicable. The ICC is valid for five years and is free to RYA members.

If you need more information on the documentation required to take a British Ship abroad visit our Going Foreign FAQ on the website.

More information on the regulations for taking British registered boats abroad can be found in the RYA books, *Foreign Cruising Vols 1 & 2*, which are available from our online shop at www.rya.org.uk/shop or telephone the orders line on 0845 345 0372.

# RYA Membership

**Promoting and Protecting Boating**
www.rya.org.uk

# RYA Membership

## Promoting and Protecting Boating

The RYA is the national organisation which represents the interests of everyone who goes boating for pleasure.

The greater the membership, the louder our voice when it comes to protecting members' interests.

Apply for membership today, and support the RYA, to help the RYA support you.

### Benefits of Membership

- Access to expert advice on all aspects of boating from legal wrangles to training matters
- Special members' discounts on a range of products and services including boat insurance, books, videos and class certificates
- Free issue of certificates of competence, increasingly asked for by everyone from overseas governments to holiday companies, insurance underwriters to boat hirers

- Access to the wide range of RYA publications, including the quarterly magazine
- Third Party insurance for windsurfing members
- Free Internet access with RYA-Online
- Special discounts on AA membership
- Regular offers in RYA Magazine
- ...and much more

**Join now - membership form opposite**

## Join online at www.rya.org.uk

Visit our website for information, advice, members' services and web shop.

**1** **Important** To help us comply with Data Protection legislation, please tick *either* Box A or Box B (you must tick Box A to ensure you receive the full benefits of RYA membership). The RYA will not pass your data to third parties.

**A.** I wish to join the RYA and receive future information on member services, benefits (as listed in RYA Magazine and website) and offers. ☐

**B.** I wish to join the RYA but do not wish to receive future information on member services, benefits (as listed in RYA Magazine and website) and offers. ☐

## When completed, please send this form to: RYA, RYA House, Ensign Way, Hamble, Southampton, SO31 4YA

**2**

| | Title | Forename | Surname | Date of Birth (D D / M M / Y Y) | Male | Female |
|---|---|---|---|---|---|---|
| 1. | | | | | ☐ | ☐ |
| 2. | | | | | ☐ | ☐ |
| 3. | | | | | ☐ | ☐ |
| 4. | | | | | ☐ | ☐ |

Address

Town | County | Post Code

Evening Telephone | Daytime Telephone

email

Signature: _____ Date: _____

**3** **Type of membership required:** *(Tick Box)*

☐ **Personal** Before 1 October 2005 annual rate £33 or £30 by Direct Debit
From 1 October 2005 annual rate £37 or £34 by Direct Debit

☐ **Under 21** Before 1 October 2005 annual rate £11 *(no reduction for Direct Debit)*
From 1 October 2005 annual rate £12 *(no reduction for Direct Debit)*

☐ **Family\*** Before 1 October 2005 annual rate £50 or £47 by Direct Debit
From 1 October 2005 annual rate £56 or £52 by Direct Debit

\* Family Membership: 2 adults plus any under 21s all living at the same address

**4** Please tick ONE box to show your main boating interest.

| | |
|---|---|
| ☐ Yacht Racing | ☐ Yacht Cruising |
| ☐ Dinghy Racing | ☐ Dinghy Cruising |
| ☐ Personal Watercraft | ☐ Inland Waterways |
| ☐ Powerboat Racing | ☐ Windsurfing |
| ☐ Motor Boating | ☐ Sportsboats and RIBs |

Please see Direct Debit form overleaf

# Instructions to your Bank or Building Society to pay by Direct Debit

Please complete this form and return it to:
Royal Yachting Association, RYA House, Ensign Way, Hamble, Southampton, Hampshire SO31 4YA

**Originators Identification Number**

| 9 | 5 | 5 | 2 | 1 | 3 |

To The Manager: _____ Bank/Building Society

Address: _____

_____

Post Code: _____

**5. RYA Membership Number (For office use only)**

**2. Name(s) of account holder(s)**

_____

_____

**6. Instruction to pay your Bank or Building Society**

Please pay Royal Yachting Association Direct Debits from the account detailed in this instruction subject to the safeguards assured by The Direct Debit Guarantee.

I understand that this instruction may remain with the Royal Yachting Association and, if so, details will be passed electronically to my Bank/Building Society.

**3. Branch Sort Code**

| | | — | | | — | | |

**4. Bank or Building Society account number**

| | | | | | | | |

Signature(s) _____

_____

Date _____

Banks and Building Societies may not accept Direct Debit instructions for some types of account

Office use / Centre Stamp

**Cash, Cheque, Postal Order enclosed** £ _____
Made payable to the Royal Yachting Association

**Office use only:** Membership Number Allocated

077